VENICE

COMPLETE GUIDE TO THE WHOLE CITY

Published and printed by

NARNI – TERNI

TEXT: LORETTA SANTINI
ENGLISH VERSION BY BRIAN WILLIAMS & ADRIAN COOK
FOTOGRAFIE: ARCHIVIO PLURIGRAF
CAMERAPHOTO ARTE - DAL MAGRO - BARONE - ARTE VIDEO

AN OVERALL VIEW

Venice is one of the best-known and best-loved cities of the world. The reason for this lies in the extraordinary beauty of its monuments and its art treasures, and in its history. But above all, it is to be found in the special quality which is reflected in the waters of its canals and side-channels, with the churches and palaces scattered around dozens of islands and islets in the Lagoon. Venice lives its life in an atmosphere of enchantment and fable, with a touch of melancholy added.

What astonishes the visitor most of all is the strange image of a duplicated city: its churches and monuments are seen reversed in the waters of the canals, and become evanescent, shifting, ever-changing. They line the banks of the Grand Canal, following its broad sinuous curves with their facades of the finest lace-like carving. Silence permeates the rios and calle, and the most secluded little squares of the city.

The enchanted fascination of the rich architecture or the mosaics of San Marco shimmering in the sun, and the magnificent mansions such as the Doges' Palace, or the Ca' d'Oro or the Ca' Pesaro, gives the city an air of opulent splendour, and causes it to gleam and sparkle. And the Rialto Bridge, the Bridge of Sighs, the superb architecture of Longhena, Sansovino and Scarpagnino, the great paintings of Tiepolo, Tintoretto and the delicate work of Bellini, the sculptures of the Lombardos, the decorations in the

Piazza San Marco and the Piazzetta: viewed from the air.
Considered one of the most beautiful squares in the world, surrounded by splendid monuments of which the most out-standing is certainly the Basilica of San Marco, the Piazza is also the religious and historic heart of Venice.

Sunset over the Basin of San Marco. The evening light heightens the rose marble of the Doges' Palace and the delicate Gothic tracery on the Venetian houses.

full flower of Gothic art, all go to make Venice one of the unique and unforgettable cities of the world.

BRIEF HISTORICAL NOTES.

The Venetian lagoon was inhabited from the 5th century of the Christian era, when as a result of the barbarian invasions, the peoples of the hinterland were forced to take refuge on the thousands of little islands which face out to the Adriatic. Here they built a community under the leadership of a 'Dux' (to be known as the

Doge in the future), who was initially chosen by the Emperor, and was subject to him. From the eighth century onwards, however, the Doge came to be chosen by popular assemblies, and this opened the way to the political and institutional autonomy of the city.

It was from this period that the fortunes of the future Republic of Venice began: from the tenth to the eleventh centuries, thanks to its strategic geographical position, and the skill and initiative of its inhabi-

tants, the city became the centre of trade in the Adriatic, and later the queen of the trade-routes to the East, assuming the role of a front rank mercantile power. This meant that enormous riches flowed in. It was then that Venice built the splendid monuments which are its chief characteristic today: the finest churches and the grandest palazzi rose, and this was the moment of the greatest creative flowering of painters, sculptors and architects.

The sea and the trade routes were

the very life of Venice. Marco Polo, merchant-venturer, embodies better than anyone the characteristics of the people of the city. Having reached China and lived there for some time, he was to narrate in "Il Milione" the story of his travels and the customs of that land.

From the sixteenth century onwards the maritime role of the city diminished, as the main focus of trade was turned from the East to the West. Despite this, the Republic would always have a leading place in the economy and history of the Italian peninsula.

It was to remain independent until 1799, when as a result of the Treaty of Campoformio it became part of the Kingdom of Lombardy and Venetia, and was then ceded to Austria. From 1866 onward, it became part of the new united Kingdom of Italy.

PIAZZA SAN MARCO

This is the religious, historical and social centre of the city. At one time it was also its political hub.

Thanks to its harmonious elegance, its beauty and its monuments, it is rightly considered the great "salotto" of Venice. It is a very large area, trapezoidal in shape and measuring 175.50 metres (nearly 580 feet) in length and 82 (266 feet) in width. Its natural continuation is in the nearby Piazzetta San Marco, which lies between the Doges' Palace, the Libreria and the Pier.

The piazza took on its present shape in the sixteenth century, when the architect Sansovino drew up its basic design. It is closed in on its longer sides by the Old Law Courts and the Clock Tower on the one hand, and by the New Law Courts on the other. On the shorter sides stand the so-called "New Building" or former Royal Palace, and above all the stupendous Basilica of San Marco flanked by the massive Campanile.

THE CAMPANILE OF SAN MARCO AND SANSOVINO'S LOGGETTA.

Almost 100 metres high, this splendid tower stands beside the Basilica of San Marco. Built towards the end of the ninth century, it was extended in height in the twelfth, and rebuilt several times, being completed at the

---

Opposite page: *Piazza San Marco. The mighty Campanile dominates the Basin of San Marco. Immediately below stands Sansovino's elegant Loggetta.*

Panoramic view of the city of Venice: in the foreground, the splendid domes of San Marco Basilica.

beginning of the sixteenth century. In 1902 it suffered a disastrous collapse, and was rebuilt a few years later as an exact replica of the original.

The architecture shows the various phases of its construction: it has Romanesque elements in the lower section, and Renaissance features in the upper part. On the topmost point stands a gilded Angel, which turns on its own axis.

The bells which once occupied the belfry of the campanile had various names according to the notes that they were destined to give out, for example the principal hours of the day or the sentences of the Court. The ascent to the top of the campanile (which has a conveniently designed spiral staircase and a lift) provides the chance to enjoy a broad panorama over Venice and its lagoon.

THE LOGGETTA OF SANSOVINO

Standing at the foot of the Campanile, and a real gem of Renaissance architecture, the loggetta was designed by Sansovino in the early part of the 16th century. The front is punctuated by three rounded arches flanked by columns. Lower down there is a balustrade which is mirrored in the attic section. Fine bronze statues of Minerva, Apollo, Mercury and Peace have been inserted into the niches, and the marble ornaments decorating the upper front section are very fine.

THE CLOCK TOWER

Built to a design by Codussi towards the end of the fifteenth century, it is famous for the two Moors which strike the hours on the great bell.

The clock is made up of a quadrant which indicates the movement of the sun and the moon and the signs of the Zodiac. When the hour strikes, a procession of figures made up of Angels and Wise Men bows towards the Madonna and Child.

Opposite page: *View of the Piazzetta, with the island and church of San Giorgio in the background.*

Sansovino's Loggetta and the Campanile seen from the Piazzetta. The Campanile collapsed in 1902 and was rebuilt shortly after using the same material.

A flight of pigeons across Piazza San Marco: view of the Basilica and the Campanile.

Panoramic view of Piazza San Marco and the buildings of the Procuratie Vecchie, the Procuratie Nuove and the Napoleonic Wing.
This is the only square in the city called "Piazza": the other squares are known as "campi" and "campielli".

THE BASILICA OF SAN MARCO

The Church is of exceptional beauty and richness of decoration. It is also one of the most fascinating architectural masterpieces of the ancient world. It is the product of an ensemble of styles and artistic elements from different periods.

HISTORY

The Church was built in the mid-eleventh century to enshrine the body of the Evangelist St Mark, which had been brought to Venice in the year 829. Previously another building had stood on the site, and this in turn had replaced an even more ancient one, destroyed by a fire. The consecration took place in 1094. From that moment, the basilica waas constantly embellished with an exceptional series of works of art - a great deal of it was taken, in fact, from other ancient buildings, and the finest of all was its magnificent and unique series of mosaics. In a very few years, the church became one of the most beautiful, theatrical and grandiose basilicas of all time. The building is in the form of a Greek cross, with four domes placed above each branch, and a larger central dome at the crossing. An atrium has been added to the front, which continues around the two sides as far as the transversal wings.

The style of the Basilica has a strong Byzantine flavour, but Romanesque and Renaissance architecture also play their part, and this mingling, together with the rich decoration, renders the overall effect absolutely unique. The architect of the building is unknown. However, it is certain that the complex was the product of constant labour by artists and mastercraftsmen, who each contributed, in his own sector, to the splendour of this basilica, and despite the diversities of style, to giving it a unity in conception.

THE FACADE

The facade stands out for the magnificence of its architecture, the splendour of the mosaics as they glitter in the sun, and the perfect delicacy of the filigree decorations which frame

The inscriptions within the mosaic read:

VISITAT INFERNVM REGNVM PRO DANDO SVPERNVM · PATRIBVS ANTIQVIS DIMISIS CHRISTVS NOVIS

QVIS FRACTIS PORTIS, SPOLIAT ME CAMPIO FORTIS

The facade is articulated by 5 great doorways beneath a row of 5 arches. Four lunettes are filled with mosaics against a gold background showing episodes from the New Testament. The great central arch is filled by a big glass window and the magnificent bronze Horses.

San Marco Basilica: a masterpiece of medieval art. Here we find styles ranging from the Byzantine, the Gothic to the Renaissance. Its architecture is greatly influenced by eastern art.

every element and rise to a climax in the crowning of the arches.

The lower part

Five great doorways open from the facade, the central one being the tallest. They are adorned with clusters of marble columns, which give a strong effect of mobility. The bas-reliefs which decorate them (especially those of the central door) are absolute masterpieces of Romanesque carving, and recount *Sacred histories,* and *Episodes of everyday life, the Months, and the Occupations of Mankind.*

The final arch, towards the south, has been closed off in order to create the Zen Chapel and the Baptistery.

The Upper part

This repeats the five arches of the lower order. The central arch, taller again than the others, has a window which illuminates the interior of the Basilica. This is where the group of *Four Horses* in bronze is to be found, a masterpiece of Greek sculpture of the 4th-3rd centuries BC. They were brought to Venice in 1204 by Doge

Enrico Dandolo, after the (Venetian) conquest of Constantinople. The *Chariot* has on several occasions been removed from Venice because of its value and beauty; Napoleon ordered it to be carried off to Paris in 1798 in order to place it in front of the Tuileries. In the arch flanking the central one are four great mosaics created in the sixteenth century to the design of Maffeo da Verona. They portray: *The Deposition of Christ from the Cross, the Descent into Hell; The Resurrection of Christ, The Ascension into Heaven.*

The sculptures of the upper section are among the most important masterpieces of Gothic art. On the summit of the Basilica is the statue of *St Mark,* and the *Lion of Saint Mark.*

South Side

This repeats the pattern of the facade, with its fine rows of arches one above the other. Here can be seen the so-called *Acritan Pilasters,* their title deriving from the fact that they were brought to Venice from San John of Acre after the victory over Genova

there in 1256. They are priceless examples of Syrian art of the sixth century. The group of the *Tetrarchs* should also be noted: two pairs of warriors, almost certainly portraying the Emperors Diocletian, Maximilianus, Valerius and Constans. This is a fourth century work, probably Syrian, though some ascribe it to Egypt.

Northern Side

This differs from the facade in decoration. The *Porta dei Fiori,* decorated in a quite sophisticated style, deserves special notice.

Right hand page: Basilica of San Marco: The Tetrarchs. *This is one of the most famous and interesting sculptural groups. The statues are made of marble which may have originated in Syria. The two pilasters at the sides are masterpieces of Syrian art of the 6th century.*

Page 18: The Clock Tower: *built to a design by Codussi towards the end of the 15th century, it is famous for the two moors which strike the hours on the great bell.*

Procession of the Cross in Piazza San Marco: Gentile Bellini (1496): a work of great beauty now in the Accadem *one of the most moving moments of the religious ceremonies which are held in Venice's central square to honour th* *Cross.*

The Bronze Horses of the Basilica.
The statues were brought to Venice by Enrico Dandolo as booty after the conquest of Constantinople.

Left-hand page: Clock Tower: the Moors which strike the hours.
The clock is made up of a quadrant which indicates the movement of the sun, and the moon and signs of the Zodiac. When the hour strikes, figures of angels and wise men bow towards the Madonna and Child.

Façade of the Basilica of San Marco: mosaic beneath the Arch of Sant'Alipio. It is the most ancient in the Basilica, and shows the "Transportation of the body of St. Mark".

The facade of the Basilica: the great doorway. The decoration is very rich: the arches are adorned with 13th century bas- reliefs. The one in the middle has representations of the Arts and Crafts. In the lunetta the mosaic shows Christ in Glory (19th century).

The Atrium

The impact of this area is stunning thanks to the effect of the magnificent mosaic decoration, the sequence of marble colonnades, and the decorative elegance which gives it its overall and unforgettable appeal. The area is characterised by slightly pointed arches, resting on columns and interspersed with six small domes. The mosaic pavement is particularly fine; created in the twelfth century, it has geometric motives in repeating circular form.

A red stone placed under the second row of columns indicates the place where, according to tradition, the Emperor Frederick Barbarossa knelt before Pope Alexander III. The most significant work is the complex of *mosaics*, which completely cover the ceiling. These feature the *Stories of the Old Testament*, and of special interest are those of the first bay, the *Genesis Stories*, created in the first years of the thirteenth century. Also in the same bay is the *Door of San Clemente*, in bronze, with bas-reliefs portraying Saints, and remarkable capitals representing animals (which surmount the columns at the sides of the door). In the other bays and in the arcades, figures of *Apostles*, *Stories from the New Testament and figures of Saints* are added to the *Stories from the Old Testament*. Great artists from all epochs have worked on the mosaic designs. There are also a number of funerary monuments dedicated to some of the Doges of Venice. The right wing has been closed in to form the Baptistery and the Zen Chapel, which are entered from the interior of the church. The left wing of the Atrium opens at the far end through the splendid *Porta dei Fiori - the Floral Door*, decorated with elegant floral bas-reliefs.

Interior

The sight of the interior can take the breath away. The overall effect of the gold of the mosaics, the interweaving of the architectural structures and the decoration which accompanies each element is unforgettable. Everything is harmonised in an atmosphere

Opposite page: *Atrium of the Basilica of San Marco. It is formed by seven abutments divided by arches. The pavement, the upper part and the domes are all decorated with mosaics.*

Below: *Porch, Dome of the Creation. The mosaics here are among the most interesting in the Basilica and also the most ancient. The various squares illustrate the Creation of the world.*

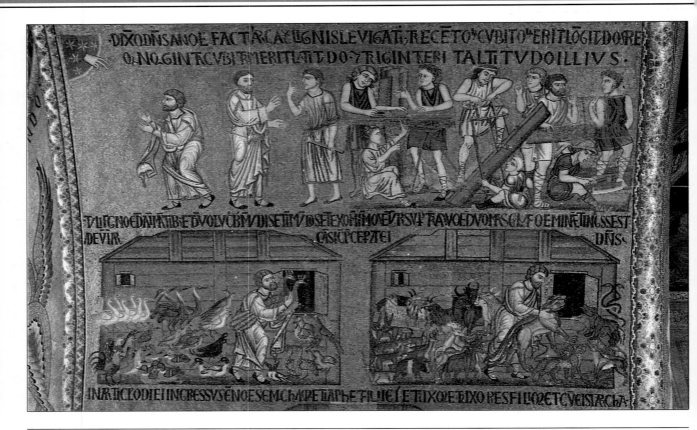

San Marco Basilica: the mosaics in the porch. The photograph shows details of the Flood and the Story of Noah.

Below: *mosaic showing "Saint Mark warns the sleeping boatman that the ship bearing his relics is approaching the estuary" (13th century).*

Detail of the mosaics in the Porch: the Tower of Babel.

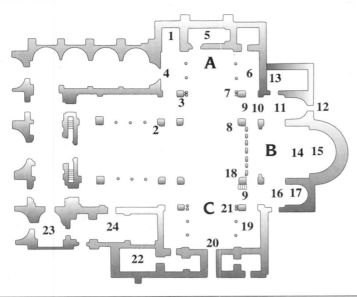

A - LEFT TRANSEPT
B- PRESBYTERY
C- RIGHT TRANSEPT

1 - Chapel of the Madonna dei Mascoli
2 - Capital of the Crucifix
3 - Holy Water stoup
4 - Door of the Madonna
5 - Chapel of St Isidore
6 - Chapel of the Madonna di Nicopeia
7 - Altar of St Paul
8 - Double ambo
9 - Iconostasis
10- Crypt of St Mark
11- Chapel of St Peter
12- Sacristy
13- Ex Church of St Theodore
14- Great Altar
15- The Pala d' oro
16- Chapel of St Clement
17- Tabernacle of the Reliquaries
18- Ambo of the Reliquaries
19- Altar of the Sacrament
20- Door
21- Altar of St James
22- Treasury
23- Zen Chapel
24- Baptistry

Interior of the San Marco Basilica: because of the splendour of its mosaics the church was called the "Golden Basilica". The surfaces are entirely covered with mosaics.

Interior of San Marco Basilica: view of the Presbytery area and the great Iconostasis.

redolent of fairyland, and the gold and marble which cover every surface give mystery and grace to the severe rhythm of the arches and vaults.

It has rightly been referred to as the *"Golden Basilica"* because gold is the dominant element in the decoration. It creates refractions, reflections, dazzling gleams which affect every part of the space, rendering it unreal and almost unlimited. We only need to remember that the mosaic cycle alone covers 4000 square metres, and that there are more than 500 columns.

The plan of the building is a Greek cross with domes for each branch of the cross and a great central dome at the crossing. The floor, of variegated marbles, is made up of geometrical patterns. The lower section of the walls of the basilica is entirely covered with rare marble, and the columns which divide the church into naves are surmounted by fine capitals in bas-relief work.

THE CHAPELS AND PRESBYTERY: LEFT TRANSEPT (A).

Chapel of the Madonna dei Mascoli (1)

This takes its name from the Confraternity of the Mascoli (its members were exclusively male). It has a Gothic altar built by Giovanni Bon in the first years of the fifteenth century, crowned by marble statues. The mosaics are of particularly great interest here because they mingle the style of the Venetian school with that of the Renaissance. They portray *Stories in the Life of the Virgin Mary*, and were created on the basis of drawings by famous artists such as Andrea del Castagno, Giambono and Jacopo Bellini.

- Chapel of the Crucifix (2) a complex of white and black columns surmounted by gilded capitals in the Byzantine style, which in turn hold up blocks of agate stone.

- Holy Water Stoup (3) - a Romanesque work of the twelfth century.

- Doorway of the Madonna (4)

- Chapel of St Isidoro (5): this was built in the fourteenth century on the orders of Doge Dandolo, to honour St Isidore, whose remains were placed here in the sarcophagus of the main altar. They had been transported to Venice in 1125. Magnificent mosaics of the 14th century decorate the chapel; they are among the most interesting in the Basilica because of the linear rhythm of the scenes represented and their narrative freshness. They tell S*tories of the life of* St Isidoro.

- Chapel of the Madonna of Nicopeia (6): so-called because of the venerated Byzantine image of the *Victorious Virgin*, transported to Venice by Doge Enrico Dandolo in the first years of the thirteenth century. It is a work of rare value, covered with gold and studded with precious stones. There is also a fine Renaissance altar.

- The Altar of St Paul (7): an elegant Renaissance work, carved by Pietro Lombardo and pupils of his school.

Opposite page: Detail of the Pala d'oro: Christ in the act of blessing, the central figure of the Pala.

Below: The Pala d'oro: a suberb monument wrought in gold at the beginning of the 10th century (3.5 x 1.40 metres). It is set with thousands of precious stones.

- **Double Pulpit** (8): so-called because it is made up of two pulpita, one above the other. Built in the fourteenth century, it consists of a lower part with an octagonal base and an upper one divided into sections and completed by columns supporting a small dome. The sculptures are works from the thirteenth century.

THE PRESBYTERY (B)

It stands over the crypt, and is separated from the rest of the Basilica by a large and magnificent iconostasis (9). This is a marble screen made up of a sequence of eight columns surmounted by capitals shimmering with gold, and by a row of statues (carved by Dalle Masegne), towards the end of the fourteenth century. It is a most exceptional example of Gothic art, and a masterpiece of Venetian sculpture.
-**The Crypt of San Marco** (10): it stands below the Presbytery, and contains the body of St Mark, patron of the city. It is divided into short naves with low columns and cross vaulting.
- **The Chapel of San Pietro** (11): has an iconostasis of marble statues made by the Dalle Massegne family. It is enriched by mosaics of the thirteenth century, a Gothic tabernacle, and a number of bas-reliefs.
- **The Sacristy** (12): a Renaissance room, decorated with mosaics based on designs by Titian and il Padovanino.
- **Former Church of San Teodoro** (13): once the Chapel of the Holy Office. Here one can see a work by Tiepolo, portraying the *Adoration of Jesus*. **High Altar**(14): in a richly decorated urn the body of St Mark is preserved here. Above four alabaster columns stands a ciborium, a thirteenth century work decorated with bas-reliefs figuring *Stories from the Gospels*. The bronze statues situated at the sides are by Jacopo Sansovino and Girolamo Paliari.
- **The Golden Altarpiece** (15): this is one of the most valuable works of the whole Basilica of San Marco. It is a huge work of gold craftsmanship, studded with precious stones. Made in the tenth century on the orders of Doge Orseolo by Byzantine and Venetian artists, it was completed and added to in the two subsequent centuries, then reassembled in its various parts by Gian Paolo Boninsegna, in 1345. The Golden Altarpiece spreads over a surface of about 3.5 metres (over 11 feet) in length, and the height is 1.4 metres (4.5 feet). It is made up of as many as 1300 pearls, hundreds of gems such as emeralds, sapphires, amethysts and rubies, and enamels and cameos.
- **The Chapel of San Clemente** (16): characterised by an iconostasis in red marble, surmounted by statues carved by the Dalle Massegnes, representing the *Madonna and Child and other Saints*. The mosaics date from the twelfth century.
- **Tabernacle of the Relics** (17): This is an elegant Gothic structure and is decorated by statues and polychrome marbles.
- **The Ambo of the Reliquary** (18): A magnificent pulpit in rare marble, made in the fourteenth century but with parts coming from much more ancient Byzantine structures. It has a polygonal base resting on columns. It was from this pulpit that the faithful were shown the relics. The decorations, featuring *peacocks* are Byzantine and date from the tenth century.

RIGHT WING OF THE TRANSEPT(C)

- **Altar of the Blessed Sacrament** (19): this was built of rare marbles in the seventeenth century. It holds the *Relics of the True Cross*.
At the fare end of this wing is the **Door** (20) which gives access to the Doges' Palace. There is a fine rose window placed above it, made even more elegant by decoration with small columns.
- **The Altar of San Giacomo** (21): A Renaissance work dating from the mid-fifteenth century.
-**The Treasury** (22): Here a large number of precious objects have been gathered together, along with reliquaries of very high artistic merit. Some of them are masterpieces of the goldsmith's art.
The Zen Chapel (23):
This is the Chapel of Cardinal G.B.Zen, buried here in the fifteenth century (his burial monument is in the centre of the chapel). He had left his vast accumulated patrimony to Venice and to the Basilica. The statue of the *Madonna della Scarpa* carved by Antonio Lombardo in 1515 and placed on the altar is of high interest; it is so-called because there is a tradition which says that a simple cloth shoe left as an offering to the Madonna by a poor man was changed into gold.
The mosaics represent *The Madonna and Child* and *Christ and the Prophets* (end of the 13th century).

THE BAPTISTERY (24).

The area is divided into three parts. At the centre stands the *Baptismal Font*, carved in the sixteenth century by Sansovino. Around it are various tombs, among them that of Doge Andrea Dandolo (built by De Sanctis), who was the patron responsible for the decoration of the place.
Among the mosaics, one the finest is above the altar portraying *Doge Dandolo adoring Christ on the Cross*. Other mosaics, mostly created in the mid-fourteenth century, recount *Stories of the Life of Christ*, *Stories of the Madonna*, and *Stories of St John Baptist*. In the Baptistery there is also the tomb of Jacopo Sansovino.

THE MOSAIC CYCLE

They almost entirely cover the walls of the Basilica, and form a complex of inestimable historical and artistic value. They cover more than 4000 square metres, and taken together they form a vast portrayal of the history of the Church.
Mosaics of the Atrium:
Old Testament Stories, *Cain and Abel*; *The Stories of Noah, the Great Flood*; *The Apostles*, *Stories from the New Testament*; *The drunkenness of Noah*; *The Tower of Babel*; *Stories of Abraham*; *Justice*; *Stories of Joseph*; *Charity*; *Stories of Joseph*; *Saints*; *Stories of Joseph*; *Saints*; *Stories of Moses*.

Opposite page: Basilica of San Marco: the Baptistry.
The baptistry is decorated with fine mosaics (14th century) and a baptismal font by Sansovino whose tomb is also here.

INTERIOR OF THE BASILICA

Mosaics of the upper part of the Church:
Arch of Paradise; the *Church Triumphant, the Exaltation of the Cross; the Triumph of the Blessed; the Damnation of the Sinners* (cartoons were by Tintoretto and Maffeo da Verona):

Arch of the Apoocalypse: *Stories from the Apocalypse and visions of the end of the world.*

Dome of Pentecost: *The Preaching of the Apostles, and the Feast of Pentecost* (a fine mosaic placed at the centre of the scene), *The Conversion of the Multitudes.*

Under the Arch: *Stories of the Passion of Christ*, a valuable thirteenth century mosaic, among the most interesting in the whole Basilica.

Dome of the Ascension: *The Ascension of Christ among the Angels and the Apostles* (13th century).

Beneath the Arch: *The Life of Christ, The Washing of Feet, The Last Supper, The Temptations of Christ, Entry to Jerusalem, the Eternal Father.*

Dome of San Leonardo, or of the Blessed Sacrament: *Saints* (13th & 14th centuries).

Beneath the Arch of the Dome of San Leonardo: *Miracles of Jesus*. made in the 18th century, they surround a fine Gothic rose window.

Presbytery (beneath the arch): *Stories of Jesus* (drawings by Tintoretto).

Dome of the Presbytery: *The Church as foreseen by the Prophets* (12th to 13th centuries).

Beneath the Arch: *The Lamb of God*

Apse: *Christ in the act of blessing, Prophets and Saints*. This may be the oldest of all the mosaics.

Beneath the left Transept Arch: *The Life of Christ* and some *miraculous episodes* (cartoon designs by Tintoretto and Veronese).

Dome of San Giovanni Evangelista: *Stories of Saint John the Evangelist* (13th century).

Beneath the Transept Arch: *Episodes in the life of Christ.*

Mosaics in the lower part of the Church:

Christ blessing (13th century).

Saints (13th century mosaics): one of the most significant examples of the Venetian School.

Cain and Abel Venetian art of the 12th century.

Chapel of the Madonna of Nicopeia: *Madonna with Saints*

Chapel of Sant'Isidoro: *Episodes in the life of St.Isidore*, an amazing work of the fourteenth century.

Chapel of the Mascoli: *Episodes in the Life of Mary*, among the most outstanding works of the fifteenth century.

Prophets; 5 absolute masterpieces of Gothic art.

Other mosaics, to be found in the nave and the smaller domes, may be observed from the galleries of the Church.

From the Basilica, we go out into Piazza San Marco.

Opposite page: *Baptistry: detail of mosaics: Salome's Dance.*
Below: *Baptistry: the mosaics showing a 14th century Crucifixion.*

Baptistry: Details of 14th century mosaics: St Luke and St Matthew.

San Marco Basilica: the facade. Sunshine reflecting on the surfaces of the Basilica brings out the gold of the mosaics, creating particularly beautiful light effects.

View of Doges' Palace and the Basilica domes.

Opposite page: View of the Venetian lagoon with the church of San Giorgio seen from the Piazzetta.
We also notice the column with the statue of the Lion of St Mark , the symbol of Venice. On the other column stands the statue of St Theodore.

Following pages: gondolas moored to the edge of the Giudecca.

PROCURATIE VECCHIE
OLD LAW COURTS

These were the meeting places of the "Procurators", or civil magistrates, of Venice, and their building was begun in the fifteenth century, by the architect Codussi. Their main feature is a long portico of 50 arches, surmounted by a double loggia of 100 arches.

PROCURATIE NUOVE
NEW LAW COURTS

This building was constructed when it was decided to move the seat of the Procurators of San Marco from the old building. Designed by Vincenzo Scamozzi, it was completed by Baldassari Longhena at the beginning of the eighteenth century. Beneath the portico there is the famous Caffé Florian, the haunt of the cultural élite since the eighteenth century.

NAPOLEONIC WING

Also known as the New Building, it is characterised by 40 arches of two orders, built in 1807 on the area formerly occupied by the church of San Geminiano, in the same style, which dated from the end of the sixteenth century. The Correr Museum is situated in this building.

THE CORRER MUSEUM

The Museum takes its name from Teodoro Correr, an indefatigable collector or pictures, books, prints, precious objects and relics of antiquity found in the monasteries, churches and abandoned houses. The collection, of great value, was given to Venice in 1830. Subsequently the city itself added to it, thanks to numerous donations and to a series of purchases. This very variegated collection provides a kind of journey through the history and art of Venice. It is divided into sections:

1st floor

In the Neo-classical Rooms there is a collection of statues by A.Canova. This is followed by the Historical collection which, together with the Collection of Renaissance Bronzes, and that of the Crafts, Trades and Games, provides rich doumentation of the Republic of Venice. There are views of the city, by means of which it is possible to reconstruct its development over the years. Then there are banners, arrases, items of clothing with the famous "doges' cap", portraits of doges, paintings of historical episodes, coins, seals, arms of various types, nautical maps and also objects of Venetian craftsmanship, such as lace, majolica, bronzes and goldsmiths' work.

2nd Floor

Apart from the Museum of the Risorgimento which contains historical items relating to major episodes of the 19th century, this floor also contains the Art Gallery known as the Quadreria.
The paintings are displayed according to period, beginning with the Byzantine age, which offers an overall view of the style of Venetian artists of the thirteenth and fourteenth centuries, and going on to the room of the most famous Venetian painters such as Lorenzo Veneziano, Vivarini, lo Schiavone, and Bellini, right through to the eighteenth century painter Pietro Longhi, famous for his Views of the Lagoon. Among the most important works we should mention those of Vivarini, represented by a Madonna and Child and a St Anthony of Padua. The works by Bellini are of major interest (a Crucifixion and a Transfig-

uration, masterpieces of the art of the late fifteenth century). Also worthy of note is the beautiful *Pietà* by Antonello da Messina, who worked in Venice in the second half of the fifteenth century, a *Crucifixion* by Ugo Van der Groes, and Carpaccio's famous painting of *Le Corteggiane*.

T*he Gabinetto di Stampe e Disegni* (prints and drawings), and the I*vory Collection* are also worth a visit.

THE PIAZZETTA, AND THE DOGES' PALACE

THE PIAZZETTA

The area included between the Basilica of San Marco and the Pier is known as the Piazzetta. On the one side it is enclosed by the Doges' Palace, and on the other by the Sansovino Library. The Basin of San Marco, which is immediately in front of the piazzetta, has been the main focal point of the city since the days of antiquity, and here all the most important buildings of the historic

Opposite page: T*he Paglia Bridge and the Prisons.*

Below: T*he Vogalonga*

centre grew up. At the beginning of the Piazzetta there are two columns from the twelfth century, on the tops of which stand the statues of the Lion of St Mark and St Theodore.

THE LIBRARY

Built by Jacopo Sansovino in the middle of the sixteenth century, it was completed later by Vincenzo Scamozzi. There is a double loggiato with columns backed by pilasters, and surmounted by an elegant balustrade, and above the cornice by statues carved by a variety of artists.

Inside, apart from the fine *Biblioteca Marciana*, there is also an Exhibition of the Library's Treasures, a collection of pictorial and sculptural work which includes paintings by Tintoretto and Titian. The staircase which leads to the floor above is particularly fine, as is the Salone, a great hall of huge proportions, designed by Sansovino and decorated with paintings and sculptures. Delicate miniatures and codexes of incalculable value are stored in glass display-cases; among them the famous *"Grimani Breviary"*, illuminated by Flemish artists. The *Mappamondo di fra' Mauro* deserves a special mention; a world-map designed in the sixteenth century, it provides a panorama of the continents known in that era, and their distribution over the earth's surface.

THE ARCHAEOLOGICAL MUSEUM

This is located behind the Sansovino Library. Formed at the end of the sixteenth century, it is one of the oldest collections of its kind in existence. Of huge proportions, it has great importance for the knowledge of Greek and Roman sculpture. The Greek originals present are the most valuable part of the Museum: among these should be mentioned the Attic statue of Athena, *the Grimani Altar*, and two works portraying a Gaul.

There are also bronzes, ceramics, epigraphs, terracottas and also vases, brooches and cameos, including a splendid *Zuleian Cameo* from the Hellenic Era.

In addition there is a collection of archaeological finds from the excavations in the islands of Torcello, Malamocco and Eracle, which were among the first in the lagoon to be inhabited.

Piazzetta San Marco.

48

THE DOGES' PALACE

This is an extraordinarily beautiful building, and one which owes its uniqueness to the effect created by its decoration and overall architectural design. The elegant finesse of the loggias, the pinkish colour of the surfaces, further enhanced by delicate geometrical motifs, the richness of the filigree decoration which decorates the whole building, all add up to making this palace one of the highest and most original examples of late mediaeval architecture.

The Palace was the ancient residence of the Doges of Venice, and thus it was the centre of the city's life. The building took on its present form in the fifteenth century, but its origins are much earlier. In 4 there was already a building on site, a fortress which underwent eat transformations over the years, and was rebuilt in ways which meant that it more and more lost the original character of a castle and assumed that of an aristocratic and magnificent residence.

EXTERIOR

What strikes one first of all is the chromatic effect of the building. The white marbles of the loggiato and the pink and grey ones of the central facade create a startling effect, enhanced by the actual atmosphere, which is characteristic of Venice: the reflections of the water seem to play on the colours and the delicate motifs of the wall surfaces.

The palazzo has two facades, at right angles to each other; one looks out over the Basin of San Marco, while the other faces on to the piazzetta.

The first is the older, and one can still see the balcony designed for it by Pier Paolo and Jacobello Dalle Masegne in 1404. Below runs a portico with sharply pointed arches, on low columns. Above this there is a loggiato, standing a little further back, and adorned between the arches with quatrefoil motifs.

The upper section has a broad wall surface in multicoloured stone along which there are large windows at intervals. Further up again the top section is crowned with interlaced filigree work in white marble.

There are three doors giving access to the interior of the Doges' Palace: the **Porta della Carta (A)**, which is the best known and opens on to Piazza San Marco, the **Porta del Frumento (B)** near the Pier, and the **Porta dell'Armar**, opening on to the Piazzetta and built in 1610.

Opposite page: *A capital on the corner of the Doges' Palace. The bas-relief shows the Judgement of Solomon, one of the masterpieces of Lamberti.*

Overall view with the Library (containing the Achæological Museum) on the left; on the right: the Doges' Pal

THE PORTA DELLA CARTA (A)

This was the triumphal entrance to the Doges' Palace. It is so-called because it was near this doorway that the documents required by the citizens were on sale, and because the scribes had their desks here. It was built between 1438 and 1442 by the Bon brothers, and is a magnificent example of the flowering of Gothic architecture, with friezes, pinnacles and rich ornamentation.

INTERIOR

A visit to the Palace begins at the **Porta del Frumento (B)** through which access is obtained to the interior. As from June 1996, a new and more functional museum tour has been initiated, permitting the visitor to view the recent restorations and the new rooms opened to the public; in particular the Museum of the Palace Works has been set up on the ground floor, and is of great historical and documentary interest. The *secret itineraries*, recently reorganised, and only visitable with special permission, reveal those parts of the palace which were more concerned with everyday life, and have remained outside traditional tourist visits.

GROUND FLOOR

Foscari colonnade and Courtyard (C) The enormous courtyard makes an immediate impact because of its elegance and ceremonial character, as well as for the mixture of architecture found there. It was

Porta della Carta: with the statue of the Lion of St Mark above the door.

Opposite page: *The Porta della Carta, its rich decoration is an outstanding example of florid Gothic.*

Opposite page.
Above: *Overall view of the magnificent courtyard of the Doges' Palace. In the background we see the wonderful architecture of the Foscari Arch.*

Below: *Courtyard of the Doges' Palace: the courtyard is ornamented with two bronze well-heads. The one in the photograph is the work of Alfonso Alberghetti.*

Staircase of the Giants, Doges' Palace. The grand staircase is set in the courtyard of the Palace. Its elegant monumental architecture was designed by Antonio Rizzo at the end of the 15th century.

Opposite page: *Foscari Arch, Doges' Palace. The noble, elegant architecture in Gothic-Renaissance style was created by Bregno and Rizzo.*

Doges' Palace: the loggias. The sequence of open arches facing the Basin of St Mark and the square below are one of the most beautiful examples of Gothic architecture.

GROUND FLOOR

A Porta della Carta
B Porta del Frumento
C Courtyard - Arch of
   the Foscari
D Courtyard of the Senators
E Giants' Staircase
F Museum of
   the Cathedral Works
P Staircase of the Censors

FLOOR OF THE LOGGIAS

G Sala del Bollo
H Sala della Milizia da Mar
I Sala dell'Avogaria
L Sala dello Scrigno
M Sala del Piovego
N Lower Chancellery
   (Offices)
O Golden Staircase

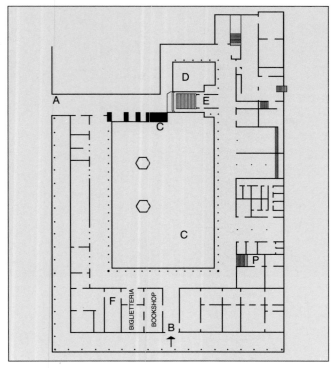

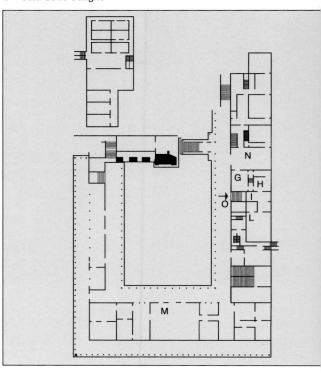

built between the fifteenth and seventeenth centuries, and all the architectural styles from Gothic to late Renaissance are represented there. In the fifteenth century Antonio Rizzo worked there, and constructed the principal facade with its double loggia. In the middle of the 16th century it was the turn of Scarpagnino, while the decoration and polychrome marbles are attributed to Pietro Lombardo. The colonnade of the courtyard was built by Bon and completed by Bregno in the middle of the fifteenth century. The **Arch of the Foscari (c)** is directly in front of the Giants' Stairway. It is typically Venetian Gothic in style. Behind the Arch is the **Courtyard of the Senators (D)**. In the centre of the space between the loggias are the two remarkable *bronze wellheads* masterpieces by Alfonso Alberghetti and Niccolò dei Conti, mid 16th century.

The Giants' Staircase (E)

This is the name given to the grand entrance to the Palace. Built towards the end of the 15th century by Antonio Rizzo, the staircase provides access to the upper loggia. The stairway is decorated with huge marble statues carved by Sansovino, and it is these which give it its name.

MUSEUM OF THE CATHEDRAL WORKS (F)

This is a group of rooms which have recently been set up: the materials on show have been distributed around the area which until the sixteenth century was the palace prison. Restoration work has revealed remains of the thirteenth century building. The most interesting collection is that of the 32 original *capitals* - those of the colonnade and those of the loggia - which once graced the Doges' residence. Some of them, especially the thirteen which came from the colonnade, have biblical and allegorical subjects and date back to the fourteenth century; the others are mainly characterised by natural decoration, or by representations of historical and religious episodes. In the Museum, various other elements of the architecture of the Palace are also preserved.

FIRST FLOOR

The Doge's Apartment

1   Scarlet Room
2   Room of the Map and the Shield
3   Grimani Room
4   Erizzo Room
5   Room of the Philosophers
6   Lion Room
7   Corner Room
8   Squires' Room
21 Passage of the Great Council
22 Great Council Chamber
23 Room of the Quarantia Civil Nuova
24 Room of the Scrutinio (Offices)
25 Armament Room or Guariento Room
26 Room of the Quarantia Civil Vecchia

SECOND FLOOR

O   Golden Staircase
9   Square Atrium
10 Room of the Four Doors
11 Room of the Anticollegio
12 Room of the Collegio
13 Room of the Senate
14 Antechapel
15 Chapel
16 Room of the Council of Ten
17 Room of the Compass
18 Room of the Three Heads
19 Room of the Head of the Inquisition
20 Armoury

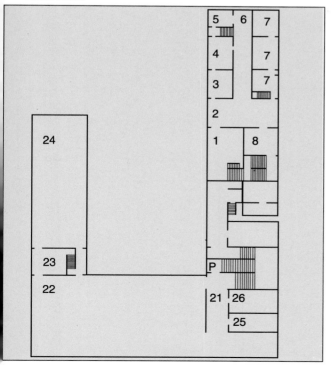

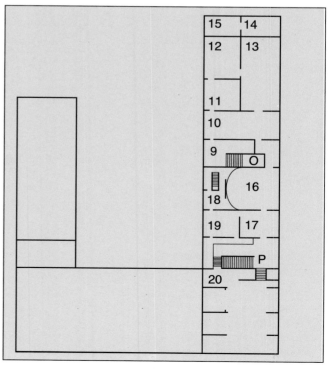

Golden Staircase (O),
Doges' Palace.
So-called because
in the upper section
it was covered
with gilded stucco-work.
It gives access to the
internal rooms.
Only the noble citizens
were allowed to use it.
It was originally conceived
by Sansovino and
designed by Scarpagnino.

The Floor of the Loggias

This is reached by the **Staircase of the Censors (P)**. The loggias are distributed along the building and along the courtyard, right up to the *Foscari Loggia*, and they enhance the harmonic effect of the building. Among the rooms of this sector, we should mention the **Sala del Bollo, the Sala della Milizia da Mar (H), the Sala dell'Avogaria(I), and the Sala dell Scrigno (L)**. The latter takes its name from the eighteenth century bureau which housed the lists of Venetian notables. Finally there are the **Sala del Piovego and the Lower Chancellery**: these were the offices of the Doges' administration.

The Golden Staircase (O)

Planned by Sansovino, and completed by Scarpagnino, this formed the elegant entrance to the internal rooms of the Palace. It is embellished with gilded stucco work, which has given it the name by which it is known.

First Floor

The Doge's Apartment.
1.*The Scarlet Room.* This takes its name from the scarlet colour of the togas worn by the Councillors who met here. It is an impressively elegant chamber, with delicate decoration by the Lombardo family, such as the *bas-relief of Doge Loredan* and the *Chimney-piece.* The gilded *wooden ceiling* is a masterpiece of the brothers Biagio and Pietro di Faenza.

2.*Room of the Maps and the Shield*: on the walls are displayed the great maps showing the world as then known, and the coat of arms of the Doge who was in office at that time.

3. *Grimani Room*: this has a fine fireplace by Lombardo.

4. *Erizzo Room*: has baroque decorations and a fireplace by Lombardo.

5. *The Room of the Stuccos*: a small chamber with very effective stucco decoration. From this room one passes out on to a terrace with a view over the Basilica of San Marco.

6. *The Room of the Philosophers*: on the walls are the portraits of the *Twelve Philosophers of Antiquity.* They were painted by Tintoretto and Veronese, and transferred here from the Library.

7. *The Doge's Own Apartment (Lion Room, Corner Room and Portrait Room)*: This is a group of three chambers with works by Bellini (*The Lamentation of Christ*) and by Carpaccio (*a Lion*), and Bosch, represented here by one of his most important paintings of religious subjects.

On the staircase leading to the floor above is a *St.Christopher*, a famous fresco by Titian.

8. The Squires' Room (to the right of the staircase): here the great canvas by Titian is to be found, depicting *Venice receiving the homage of Neptune.* There are also works by Tintoretto and Palma the Younger.

Second Floor

9.*The Square Atrium*: served as an ante-chamber. It has a very fine ceiling with works by Tintoretto, portraying Doge *Girolamo Priuli*, and

---

Right-hand page: Doges' Palace, the Room of the Maps, or of the Shield: this is decorated with a series of maps showing the areas of the word as then known. They were mostly painted in the 15th century. The two wordmaps in the centre of the room are particularly fine. On the walls were also placed the coat of arms of the Doge who was in office.

Doges' Palace: Neptune Offering Venice the Gifts of the Sea, Giovan Battista Tiepolo.

Doges' Palace, Hall of the Four Doors. Designed by Palladio the Hall takes its name from the four doors of the room. The ceiling was painted by Tintoretto, Contarini and Titian.

also by Veronese and Paolo Flammingo.

10. Room of the Four Doors: designed by Palladio, this room is so-called because four doors lead into it. The *ceiling* is painted by artists including Tintoretto, Tiepolo, Contarini and Titian, here represented by his portrait of *Doge Antonio Grimani*.

11. Room of the Anticollegio: a small chamber with frescos by Tintoretto, showing *mythological scenes*. It was rebuilt by Palladio and Vittoria after being destroyed by fire. Among the most important works, mention should be made of several masterpieces by Tintoretto (*Mercury and the Graces, Bacchus and Ariadne, Minerva and Mars*). The splendid *Rape of Europa* is by Paolo Veronese (late 16th century).

12. Room of the Collegio: This was the chamber used for the meetings of the Council. It is a very impressive room, and has a number of valuable artworks. The coffered ceiling is enriched by a masterpiece by Veronese, showing *Venus enthroned*, surrounded by symbolic representations of *the Virtues*. On the walls there are paintings with subjects from the *History of Venice*, together with portraits of a number of illustrious citizens. Among the most famous paintings is one of the *Sacred Marriage of St Catherine* by Tintoretto.

13. Room of the Senate: this too was built after the disastrous fire of 1577. The walls and ceilings are completely covered with frescos by many artists, including Tintoretto, Palma the Younger and Antonio Vincentino, showing *Episodes in the History of Venice.*

14. The antechapel: a tiny area gracefully decorated with stucco work.

15. The Chapel: completely covered in frescos, it also has sculptures by Jacopo Sansovino, including a *Madonna and Child* (on the altar).

From here we return to the Room of the Four Doors (10) and pass on to

16. The Room of the Council of Ten: copies of paintings by Paolo Veronese depicting mythological scenes are inserted into the wooden inlay ceiling.

17. Room of the Compass: this served as an antechamber to the Room of the Council of Ten. It has a fine fireplace by Sansovino, and several paintings.

18. Room of the Three Heads of the Council of Ten: (this is part of the "Secret Tour"): the ceiling is decorated by various artists, including Veronese.

19. Room of the Head of the Inquisition: (part of the "Secret Tour"): linked to the Bridge of Sighs by a secret passage, and to the Torture Chamber, it has a ceiling painted by Tintoretto.

20 The Armoury: or Room of the Weapons: it has on display a varied and interesting collection of weapons. These have always been kept in these rooms because they were used by the Councillors themselves for their own defence. Among the rarest pieces is a 'colubrina' of the 16th century, the armour once thought to belong to Gattamelata, and that of King Henri IV of France.

FIRST FLOOR

We return to the First Floor by way of the **Scala dei Censori (P)**:

21. Passage of the Great Council:. a passageway between the Room of the Council of Ten and the remainder of the Building.

22. Great Council Chamber: the pro-

Doges' Palace, Sala dell' Anticollegio: a room reconstructed by Palladio and Vittoria and frescoed by Tintoretto. Among the finest art works is Veronese's "Rape of Europa".

Doges' Palace, Sala dell' Anticollegio: "The Rape of Europa". One of Paolo Veronese's masterpieces. He toned down the brilliance of the scene and costumes to give the composition a classical effect.

portions are vast, and the blend of architecture and decoration is sumptuous. Here the 'Nobili' of Venice, inscribed in the Golden Book, used to meet. The chamber was painted with frescos by Guariento, and then, after the fire which devastated it, by the greatest artists of the City, including Bellini, Carpaccio, Veronese and Tintoretto.

The paintings:

a) *Paradise* by Tintoretto: a work of vast dimensions (7 metres by 22), especially interesting in the complexity of its composition, the play of light and shade and the extraordi-nary number of persons represented. It was painted with the help of many assistants, because the master himself by this time was quite old.

b) *Episodes in the life of Doge Sebastiano Ziani, Pope Alexander III and Frederick I Barbarossa.*

c) *Episodes in the story of Venice.*

d) Representation of the *Fourth Crusade*, and Venice's participation in this event.

On the ceiling are works by Veronese, portraying the *Apotheosis of Venice*, another of the painter's great masterpieces. The arrangement of the figures is especially striking, as is the attention paid to architectonic detail and the overall decorative taste of the work.

23.The Room of the Quarantia Civil Nuova (New Civil Court):this was the Court of appeal for civil cases. The room has 16th century decoration.

24. The Room of the Scrutinio (Election of the Doge): it possesses a *Triumphal Arch* in imitation of those of the Roman era. The paintings are by imitators of Tintoretto and Veronese. On the wall directly in front of the arch is the *Last Judgment* by Palma the Younger. The *Battle of Lepanto* was painted by Vicentino.

25. Armament Room or Guariento Room: it takes its name from the fresco by Guariento, illustrating *Paradise* (14th century). Recently restored, the painting beautifully depicts *The Coronation of the Virgin*.

26. Room of the Quarantia Vecchia (Old Court): this has decorations from the seventeenth century. It was the old Appeal Court.

PRISONS.

We come next to the ancient and sadly notorious prisons of Venice. The part which was underground was known as "*Piombi*" (the leads) because the walls were lined with strips of lead, which made them broiling and unbearable in the summer heat. The prisons which were above ground, on the other hand, were known as "*Pozzi*" (the wells) because they were subject to flooding for many days of the year, and even when this was not the case they were extremely humid. Casanova was imprisoned in the Piombi, and was involved in a wildly adventurous flight, described by him in his *Memoirs*.

Doges' Palace, Sala dell' Anticollegio: "Mars Dismissed by Pallas", by Tintoretto, one of the mythological scenes that decorate the room.

Doges' Palace, Senate Hall. A grand ceremonial room. It was rebuilt after its destruction by fire in 1547. The frescoes on the walls and ceiling were painted by Tintoretto, Palma the Younger and Antonio Vicentino. This was the room where the Senators of the Venetian Republic held their assemblies.
Below: The Lion of St Mark painted by Vittore Carpaccio.

Right: Doges' Palace, Sala del Collegio. Here the assemblies of the Council were held. It is one of the most sumptuous rooms of the Palace containing masterpieces by great artists. Among them are admirable paintings by Tintoretto and Veronese. We notice Veronese's great canvas of the "Battle of Lepanto". It stands behind the seat where the Doge of Venice presided over the meetings, and was commissioned as thanksgiving on the part of the Republic for the victory over the Turks. The other paintings show Episodes from the history of Venice and allegorical compositions. The Sala del Collegio was rebuilt after the fire which almost completely destroyed it, together with other rooms in the Palace. Its architects were Palladio and Dal Ponte.

Left: Doges' Palace, Hall of the Council of Ten: this was the seat of the Venetian Magistrature who were responsible for the City's defences.

Right: Doges' Palace, Hall of the Council of Ten.
On the walls and ceiling there we find many paintings by Paolo Veronese. The photo shows a detail of "Juno Offering her Treasures to Venice".
Below: Doges' Palace, Hall of the Three Heads of the Council of Ten: the particularly beautiful decorations on the ceiling were painted by various artists, among them Veronese.

Doges' Palace, Hall of the Great Council. This is the largest room in the Doges' Palace and was the seat of the Council of Nobles. After the fire in the 16th century it was repainted by Bellini, Carpaccio, Veronese and Tintoretto.

Below: Doges' Palace, Hall of the Great Council. "Portrait of the Doges Agostino Barbarigo and Leonardo Loredan", Domenico Tintoretto.

Doges' Palace, Hall of the Great Council. "Paradise", (detail) by Tintoretto: the work measures 7 x 22 metres. It is one of Tintoretto's masterpieces and certainly one of his most complex works because of its elaborate composition and the immense number of figures which make up the picture.

THE BRIDGE OF SIGHS.

The architecture is delicate and original in style; it was built in 1589 by Antonio Contin, and is one of the most famous bridges in the world. It was built to link the Court to the Prisons. It was known as the Bridge of Sighs because of the moans of the condemned when, after receiving their sentence, they crossed the brief tract which separated them from their cells, and saw the light of day for the last time.

The Bridge of Sighs.

Opposite page: *Island of San Giorgio, Church of San Giorgio Maggiore. The island lies in front of the Basin of St Mark. It is dominated by the grandiose white facade of the Church of San Giorgio Maggiore, one of the masterpieces of 17th century art. Designed by Palladio its interior includes works by Tintoretto and Carpaccio. The monastery buildings on the island are the seat of the Giorgio Cini Foundation, particularly distinguished for its cultural activities.*

THE ISLAND OF SAN GIORGIO

In the past this island was known as the "Isle of Cypresses" because it had a considerable area of greenery. At the end of the tenth century, on the orders of Doge Morosini, a monastery was built here. Since 1951, the Giorgio Cini Foundation has had its headquarters in this monastery; a foundation which has played a great international role in the spread of culture and in the presentation of art exhibitions of the highest level. Its activity is mainly in the study of Venetian civilisation, in the field of literature - the Library in the Foundation is one of the richest in Italy - and in art, music and theatre.

THE CHURCH OF
SAN GIORGIO MAGGIORE

This is a magnificent Palladian building: the white facade flanked by the tall, imposing tower dominates the southern side of the Bay of San Marco. Begun in the sixteenth century on the foundations of an older church dating back to the eleventh, it was completed in 1610.

It has four large columns forming a single order.

Above these is a timpanum, while beside them are the two wings corresponding to the two lateral naves inside the church. Between the columns are the main entrance, and two niches with statues of St George and St Lawrence.

The *interior* is stately and harmonious, in the form of a basilica. It is adorned with works by Bassano and Tintoretto, represented here by his masterpiece portraying *The Last Supper*, and by the so-called *Gathering of the Manna*. Another fine work is the *St.George killing the Dragon* by Carpaccio.

A work of great originality is the sixteenth century wooden choir.

The ascent of the tower is a great delight; from it an unforgettable view over the whole city can be obtained.

THE GRAND CANAL

The Grand Canal is the "main street" of Venice. With Piazza San Marco and the Doges' Palace it is the principal attraction of the city. The exceptional beauty of the buildings lining its banks, the charm of watching the slow progress of the elegant, elaborate facades reflected in the water, and the delightful jostling of gondolas and vaporettos for position , all makes a trip down the Grand Canal a wonderfully interesting experience. It is a fascinating journey through centuries of political, economic and cultural history.

The effect created by the elaborate tracery decorating the palaces reflected in the Grand Canal, and thereby multiplying the appeal of this experience, is unforgettable. The water echoes the elaborate architectural decoration, mirroring the colours of the walls into a thousand facets.

It creates a fabulous world of fantasy that touches the heart from moment to moment.

The Grand Canal winds its way in an enormous inverted "S" for almost 2 miles through the historic centre of Venice, linking Piazzale Roma to the Basin of St Mark fronting on to San Marco Basilica and the Doges' Palace.

Historically it is the nucleus of the development of the Venetian Republic.

It is here that merchandise arrived from the East to be deposited in the numerous ancient warehouses that lined the canal embankments. It was here that the aristocracy and rich merchants of Venice built their palaces.

These magnificent buildings, built in extraordinary architecture that ranges from the Romanesque to the Baroque, are the most characteristic feature of the Grand Canal.

Down the left and right hand banks of the Grand Canal stand palaces, churches and warehouses which have marked the most incisive moments of Venice's history.

The Canal is crossed by three bridges: the **Scalzi Bridge, the Ac-**cademia Bridge, and then the **Rialto** which, together with the Bridge of Sighs beside the Doges' Palace, is certainly the most famous and the best-loved bridge in the world. **Piazzale Roma**: this is the most important centre for land traffic. It marks the terminus for buses and cars arriving from the mainland and is well supplied with garages and service stations.

Near the **Santa Lucia embankment** we find the **Railway Station.**

From the **Santa Lucia wharf** vaporettos depart for various stops throughout the city.

On the right bank we find the **Papadopoli Gardens**, a small green plot with a charm of its own.

Then comes the **Church of San Simeone Piccolo** (18th century) with its familiar copper dome and the **Palazzo Diedo** (18th century) in Neo-classical style with a handsome loggia.

At the left of the **Scalzi Bridge** (designed by Eugenio Miozzi in 1934) we see the **Scalzi Church** built by Longhena in the 17th century. Its beautiful facade is ornamented with statues, niches, paired columns and a great doorway.

The interior is particularly sumptuous with its polychrome marbles, statues and busts, and Baroque altars surmounted by baldachins. The paintings are from the 17th and 18th centuries: particularly fine is

the *Santa Teresa* fresco by G.B. Tiepolo.

The **Palazzo Correr Contarini** , or Ca' dei Cuori (17th century) is interesting with its two loggias placed one above the other against the red background of the walls.

On the right bank stands the **Fondaco dei Turchi** (12th and 13th centuries), a historically important building , also much admired for its Byzantine architecture. It contains the **Natural History Museum.**

Almost opposite, on the left bank, stands the **Palazzo Vendramin Calergi** in splendid Renaissance style. The Grand Canal continues its way past noble palaces.

On the right, heading for the Rialto, it passes one of the most interesting buildings in Venice: the **Church of San Stae**.

This Baroque church was built at the beginning of the 18th century by the architect Domenico Rossi. The facade has high columns with Corinthinan capitals, a grand doorway, a huge pediment and is adorned with a group of sculptures. The interior follows classical principles with prevalently 18th century decoration.

Among the many noteworthy works of art we must not forget the beautiful *Martyrdom of St Bartholomew* (an early work by Tiepolo) and the *Martyrdom of St James* by Piazzetta. Next we come to the magnificent **Palazzo Pesaro** built by Longhena in the 17th century: it contains the Gallery of Modern Art and the Oriental Museum; then **Palazzo Corner della Regina; Palazzo Favretto** , belonging to the Bragadin family (14th century); and the **Pescheria**, a red building from the early 20th century.

A little further on we find the **Fabbriche Nuove di Rialto** built by Sansovino in the 16th century (now the Law Courts and Legal Offices), then the **Fabbriche Vecchie di Rialto**, a 16th century complex by Scarpagnino with its rows of rectan-

Panoramic view of the Dogana Point and the Church of the Salute. The Dogana Point marks the extreme end of the Grand Canal: it looks out over the Basin of St Mark.

Grand Canal: the Church of the Scalzi, built by the architect Longhena (17th century). The interior is decorated with paintings of the 17th and 18th centuries.

gular windows on two floors.
On the square in front of it a market is held.
Then comes **Palazzo Camerlenghi** with its elegant sober architecture of the Renaissance.
On the left bank of the canal we see the splendid **Ca' d'Oro,** one of the most admired and elaborately decorated palaces in Venice (inside, the **Franchetti Gallery)** and the **Ca' Da Mosto,** an elegant building in Venetian-Byzantine style.
In spite of rebuilding it still remains extremely fine because of its design and decoration.
It is the house where Alvise Da Mosto was born, the man who discovered the Cape Verde Islands.
Next comes the **Fondaco dei**

Tedeschi by the architect Scarpagnino.
The ground floor of this Renaissance building is in the form of a widely open loggia. The decorations attributed to Giorgione and Titian, which once adorned the facade, have since disappeared.
The **Rialto Bridge** connects the islands of the Venetian lagoon half way down the Grand Canal.
Famous the world over, the bridge has an open loggia type structure that follows the curve of the single arch.
Between the Rialto and Accademia Bridges we find some of the most beautiful buildings in Venice.
On the left bank we see the Renaissance **Palazzo Manin** with its great

portico on the ground floor; the 13th century **Palazzo Loredan,** now the seat of the City Council; **Palazzo Grimani,** a beautiful building with three superimposed loggias, built in the 14th century by Sanmicheli: now the seat of the Court of Appeals; **Palazzo Corner-Spinelli** , a masterpiece of the 15-16th centuries.
After a curve in the Canal we see **Palazzo Mocenigo,** a complex built in the 16th-17th centuries which combines two buildings behind a single facade; the Renaissance **Palazzo Contarini delle Figure**; **Palazzo Grassi,** one of the most prestigious in the city since it houses important art exhibitions.
On the right bank we see **Palazzo**

Papadopoli , a harmonious Renaissance building ornamented with two original obelisks.

Next comes **Palazzo Bernardo** (15th century building in Gothic style characterized by a succession of airy richly decorated arches);the late Renaissance **Palazzo Balbi** - known as the "turn of the canal" because it stands at the curve of the Grand Canal.

A little further on we see the **Ca' Foscari**, a jewel of Venetian Gothic (15th century).

Then the **Palazzo Giustinian** created from a combination of two 15th century buildings, with finely decorated windows and a handsome facade featuring three porticos one above the other; **Palazzo Rezzonico** is the seat of the Museum of 18th Century Venice.

The last stretch of the Grand Canal runs from the **Accademia Bridge** to the Basin of St Mark.

Just over the bridge in the Campo della Carità we find the buildings that house the **Accademia Gallery.** On the left bank stands the **Palazzo Cavalli Franchetti**, built in Gothic style (19th century); the handsome **Palazzo Corner** or **Ca' Grande** designed by Sansovino (16th century); the **Palazzo Contarini-Fasan** (second half of the 15th century in Venetian Gothic).

On the right bank we see **Palazzo Barbarigo, Palazzo Venier dei Leoni**, of special interest because it houses **Peggy Guggenheim's collection of contemporary art**. Then comes the striking **Palazzo Dario**, and a little further on the **Church of the Salute** and the **Dogana Point**, with its tower on which stands the statue of Fortune to mark the end of the Grand Canal.

In splendid isolation facing the Basin of St Mark rises the noble facade of the **Church of San Giorgio** on its island of the same name.

Fondaco dei Turchi and the Civic Museum of Natural History. A fine palace in Venetian-Byzantine style rebuilt in the 19th century: it is characterized by its series of loggias built one on top of the other. It houses the Civic Museum of Natural History which contains collections of great scientific interest including an entomological department (a very rich collection of insects) and one devoted to fossils and minerals. There is a well developed sector dealing with marine fauna and the one devoted to ethnography. The Museum has a Library of scientific publications.

Palazzo Vendramin Calergi. A magnificent building dating from the early 16th century by Mauro Codussi and Lombardo. The very elegant Renaissance style of the facade is reinterpreted in the spirit of Venetian architecture with handsome two-light mullioned windows which create a double portico. This is the palace where the composer Richard Wagner died.

Ca' d'Oro - Franchetti Gallery. A wonderful building because of its fusion of architectural and decorative elements, the colouring of its varied surfaces, and the delicate tracery that accompany its structural elements. It is called Ca' d'oro (golden house) because the outer surfaces were once clad in gold leaf. This palace remains one of the finest examples of Venetian-Gothic architecture of the 15th century. The entrance courtyard and a second courtyard express the same elegant architecture as the exterior. A magnificent well-head by Bartolomeo Bon stands in the centre of the courtyard. The Ca' d'Oro houses the Franchetti Gallery. This is a rich and extremely important collection of paintings together with another section devoted to medals, seals, tapestries, ceramics and antique furniture.

Above: *View of the Grand Canal from the Riva del Vin.*

Opposite page, above left: Palazzo Corner della Regina. *The 18th century palace was built over a pre-existing palace belonging to Caterina Cornaro, Queen of Cyprus.*

Above right: Palazzo Pesaro and Gallery of Modern Art. *The palace faces onto the right bank of the Grand Canal. It was built by Longhena in the 17th century. It contains the Gallery of Modern Art and the Oriental Museum. The Gallery of Modern Art is a collection of great historical value: it contains art of the 19th and 20th centuries with particular reference to Venetian trends. At present, thanks to its close connection with the Venice Biennale, it has expanded its international interests. The artists represented are among the most famous in the world. Most outstanding among the works exhibited (and the first to be acquired by the Gallery) is the "Judith" (also known as "Salome") by Gustav Klimt. The Oriental Museum. The Museum covers the upper floors of Palazzo Pesaro and is considered the largest and most important collection of oriental art in Europe. It began with the material gathered by Enrico di Borbone during his travels in the Far East towards the end of the 19th century. Since then the collection has been enlarged from time to time by donations from public and private sources.*
The Museum has a rich array of arms and armour, flags and banners, ivories, costumes, sculpture, musical instruments, textiles, ceramics, stones and shadow puppets. The screen collection is exceptional. The countries represented are China, Japan, Indochina, the Sonda Islands and India.

Below: Pescheria. *The building dates from 1907 and resumes the style of the typical Venetian palace on the Grand Canal. Built with the familiar red plastered walls, the building has an open portico on the ground floor - where the fish market is held - and another, narrower, portico on the upper floor.*

RIALTO BRIDGE.

This is one of the most typical and symbolic monuments of Venice, and one of the most justly famous all over the world. 50 (160 feet) metres long, it is built in the form of one great arch, above which, on both sides, runs a loggia which is raised to a greater height in the centre. It was built at the end of the sixteenth century by Antonio Da Ponte.

Previously there were other bridges in this stretch of the Canal. The first, a simple group of pontoons, dated from 1180; in the mid thirteenth century, it was replaced by another in wood. This fell down in 1444, and in its place yet another wooden bridge was built, which lasted until the construction of the present one.

View of the Rialto bridge and gondolas on the Grand Canal.

Scenes from the historic Regatta down the Grand Canal.
Below: The Bucintoro, the Doge's boat, advancing through the gondolas.

THE HISTORICAL REGATTA

The Regatta is the most typical and fascinating festival in Venice. It recalls the years when the city was Mistress of the Marine Republics. A procession of boats parades down the Grand Canal carrying rowers and historical personalities in period costumes. Most splendid of all is the Bucintoro, the boat used by the Doges.

THE CARNIVAL OF VENICE

A rich, sumptuous and joyous Venetian event. For days on end Venetians wearing the most beautiful and typical fancy-dress costumes parade through the city.

FESTIVAL OF THE "REDENTORE" (BELOW)

The festival was introduced as a thanksgiving to the Redeemer (Redentore) for the end of a plague epidemic in 1576. Today it is one of the most moving and theatrical events in the Venetian calendar.
Together with religious ceremonies and the procession, a number of spectacles and festivities are held; especially the splendid procession of boats hung with lights and decorations.

Palazzo Grassi
An extremely well proportioned building with grandiose and elegant architectural elements. It was built in the 18th century with the project carried to completion by Giorgio Massari. The palace houses the Arts and Costume Centre and every year holds world famous art exhibitions, conferences and cultural conventions. Some of the exhibitions linked to the Venice Biennale of Contemporary Art are held in these rooms.

Opposite page: the Grand Canal with Palazzo Giustinian.
The palace was built by combining two 15th century houses.
Elegant architectural elements articulate the porticoed storeys of the palace.

Ca' Foscari - One of the most beautiful examples of florid Gothic. The brick-coloured facade is relieved by the delicate tracery of the marble porticoes and finely decorated windows. The decoration of the loggias becomes more and more elaborate as they rise from the lower orders to the upper storey. The building dates from the early years of the 15th century.

THE CA' REZZONICO AND THE
MUSEUM OF THE VENETIAN EIGHTEENTH CENTURY

The palace was begun by Longhena in the seventeenth centuries and completed by Massari in the eighteenth. The rooms, splendidly decorated by Tiepolo and other artists, have housed the Museum of Eighteenth Century Venetian Art since 1936. The building lent itself particularly well to a faithful and accurate reproduction of the noble dwellings of the city in that era: For this reason it was restored under the auspices of the city of Venice to house furniture, hangings, carpets and works on the city's history in the 1700s. The palace is thus a luxurious and magnificent record of an historical period and of the life that was lived in houses like this by the patrician families.

There are magnificent Flemish arrasses, valuable furniture, inlaid and engraved by famous masters of the age, such as the work of Andrea Bortolon. The hangings and lamps are of the finest quality, and the rich decoration of the ceilings and plasterwork which adorn vaults and doorways are most striking in their effect.

The rooms of the palace are often further adorned by statues and bas-reliefs. There is a valuable and extensive collection of prints from the eighteenth century, and many fine pictures and frescos.

Some of the paintings are of great importance, notably the work by Gian Battista Tiepolo, entitled *Allegories* (this is to be found in the so-called Throne Room), and his *Strength and Wisdom* (in the Tiepolo Room), and also *The Marriage of Ludovico Rezzonico* in the Room of the Nuptial Allegory.

Among the paintings, a note calls attention to the 34 small pictures by Longhi portraying *Venetian Scenes* –

these are exquisite compositions, with remarkable narrative freshness. Famous and typical persons of the Venice of those days are portrayed in them, and they thus provide an insight into the society of the epoch.

In the Sala del Ridotto, there are delightful works by Guardi. He also painted some of the ceilings. The female artist Rosalba Carriera is also represented by some interesting works.

Above: Ca' Rezzonico: Ballroom. This is one of the most sumptuous palaces in Venice. The stucco decorations, tapestries and paintings are particularly beautiful. The elaborate chandeliers are exceptional.

Opposite page: Ca' Rezzonico: an 18th century building originally designed by Longhena. The interior was decorated by Tiepolo. It houses the interesting Museum of 18th Century Venice.

Right: Ca' Rezzonico, Museum of 18th Century Venice: this is in fact a faithful and valuable reconstruction of a noble Venetian house. We are able to admire the original interior decoration, furniture, paintings, ornaments and wall hangings and upholstery of the period, as well as a number of other works typical of Venice at that time in its history.

I GRECI IN OCCIDENTE

PALAZZO GRASSI VENEZIA 24 III-8 XII.1996 ORE 9-19

Above: The Accademia Bridge: one of the three bridges crossing the Grand Canal. This wooden bridge was built as one huge arch across the water.

Left: *Palazzo Corner or Ca' Grande*
Designed by Sansovino (16th century). The ground floor has three great arches while on the two upper floors there are two orders of windows alternating with half columns.

GALLERY OF THE ACCADEMIA

This is a big museum complex housing works of great historical and artistic value, ranging from the fourteenth to the eighteenth centuries. They provide a broad spectrum of Venetian painting and its evolution over the centuries. The historical nucleus of the Gallery comes from the group of paintings collected for study by the Academicians. Subsequently, it was enriched by numerous bequests, and also by a series of important purchases. It was opened to the public from 1817 onwards, and is now housed in a whole group of buildings, including the Great School, the Church of Santa Maria della Carità (15th century), and the Monastery of the (Augustinian) Canons. The collection, distributed throughout 24 rooms, tells the story of five centuries of Venetian painting, and some of the very finest works of the artists represented are on display. There are a large number of paintings by Giovanni Bellini (known as Il Giambellino), one of the greatest exponents of Venetian painting in the late fifteenth century, and the man who brought renewal to it. He was able to give the plastic quality and sense of volume peculiar to Renaissance art to his scenes and figures, but he modified the effect by his softness of line, and above all by his use of luminous, soffused colours. Among the paintings in the Gallery, we would mention especially:

-*Sacra Conversazione*, or *The Altarpice of San Giobbe*;
- *Madonna and Child and Saints Catherine and Mary Magdalene*;
- *Le Allegorie*: five small works forming part of the decoration of a piece of furniture;
- *Madonna and Child*, known as the *Madonna of the Little Trees*;
- *La Pietà*: possibly the most famous and expressive of the artist's works.
- *Head of the Redeemer*
-*Triptych of St.Lawrence*;
-*Triptych of the Madonna*
-*Triptych of St Sebastian*;
-*Triptych of the Nativity*.

Also worthy of note is the *Procession in Piazza San Marco* by Gentile Bellini, a work of exceptional expressive power.

The Venetian painting of Byzantine inspiration (14th century) is of special interest. Paolo, Lorenzo and Caterino Veneziano are all represented (*The Coronation of the Virgin* and *The Annunciation and Four Saints*, together with

Accademia delle Arti: the Art Academy houses the Accademia Gallery which exhibits works ranging from the 14th to the 18th centuries. Here we can admire some of the masterpieces of Giovanni Bellini, Lorenzo Veneziano, Carpaccio, Veronese, Titian and Giorgione.

Vittore Carpaccio: "Healing of a Man Possessed". One of the episodes from the Story of St Ursula.

Tintoretto: "St Mark Saving a Saracen".

Jacobello da Fiore, with his *Coronation of Mary*. Giorgione is represented by some of his most important paintings; justly famous is *La Tempesta* which arrests the attention because of the innovative way in which landscape is used and the remarkable use of colour. An original and exeptionally expressive painting is the portrait of *An Old Woman* by the same painter. The very beautiful *Stories of Saint Ursula* is one of the outstanding works by Carpaccio, while among the Titians, there is the *St John Baptist*, and the amazing *Pietà*, the artist's last work - full of dramatic expression and suffused with the agonised distortion of the forms. Veronese is represented by his masterpiece, *The Supper in the House of Levi*. Painted in 1573, it provides a spectacular representation, in great detail, of the costumes and the architecture of Venice in that period. There are many Tintorettos in the collection: *The Miracle of St Mark* is possibly the most important. This is made up of two canvasses, in which he stresses the dynamism of the figures, and above all the use of chiaroscuro to render the expressive

Vittore Carpaccio: "The Dream of St Ursula", an episode from the Story of St Ursula.

Paolo Veronese: "The Supper in the House of Levi". A large scale and very well composed painting. The wealth of details which characterize the scene is exceptional.

Below: Gentile Bellini: "The Miracle of the Cross at San Lorenzo".

quality of the scene more vivid. Other paintings by the same artist include *Adam and Eve*, *The Presentation of Christ in the Temple*; *Cain and Abel* and *The Deposition from the Cross*. The Gallery also displays works by Mantegna (*St George*), Cosmè Tura (a *Madonna and Child*), Piero della Francesca (*St Jerome*), Lorenzo Lotto (*Portrait of a Gentleman*), Paris Bordone (*The Giving of the Ring*) and Palma the Elder (*Sacra Conversazione*). We can also find paintings by Basaiti, Benedetto Diana, Vivarini, Sebastiano del Piombo, Pordenone and Schiavone.

Giorgione: "The Storm". This one of the Master's most famous paintings and one of the chief masterpieces of 16th century Italian art. The warm colour tones and the importance landscape assumes in the composition are particularly striking.

Above: Vittore Carpaccio. "The Return of the Ambassadors".
Below: Vittore Carpaccio: "The Meeting of Ursula and Ereo", and "Departure of the Pilgrims", from the Story of S. Ursula.

PALAZZO VENIER DEI LEONI

PEGGY GUGGENHEIM ART COLLECTION

This is one of the most important collections of contemporary art in the world, and certainly the richest and most valuable in Italy. The collection takes its name from its founder and patron Peggy Guggenheim, who owned the Palazzo.

The most important artists in the areas of cubism, futurism, dadaism, surrealism and abstractism are all represented here; there are many masterpieces by Picasso, Braque, Boccioni, Kandinksy, Mondrian, Chagall, Max Ernst, Pollock, Vedova, Pomodoro, Duchamp, De Chirico, Severini, Marcoussis, Magritte, Paul Klee and Mirò.

Palazzo Barbarigo: a handsome 19th century palace with its facade decorated scenographically with mosaics on a historical subject, by Giulio Carlini.

Below: *Palazzo Venier dei Leoni: the building houses Peggy Guggenheim's famous art collection, one of the most important for contemporary art.*

THE CHURCH OF THE SALUTE

This exceptional church, with its delicate and articulated architecture, dominates the scene at the end of the Grand Canal.

Building began in 1630, as a thankoffering to the Madonna who was believed to have brought an end to the terrible outbreak of plague. It was designed by Baldassarre Longhena, who produced a real masterpiece of baroque art.

The plan is octagonal, divided into a series of projecting sections, the largest of which acts as a facade. Opposite this is a broad and gracefully designed stairway.

The main body of the building is surmounted by an open drum with tall, deep-set windows.

Above this rises the majestic and dignified dome, culminating in a lantern.

Broad volutes link the the lower section to the upper part. Each element of the building is enriched with statues, cornices and bas-reliefs, so that the overall effect is of great richness.

A second smaller dome placed above the presbytery, and two small campaniles complete the overall scheme.

The interior is almost theatrical in effect, for the octagonal plan, the breadth of the central area, the movement bestowed by the columns and chapels, create an atmosphere of solemn grandeur.

In the Presbytery there is the High Altar, surmounted by a marble reredos figuring the Plague fleeing before the Virgin. This contains the venerated image of the Madonna della Salute, a Byzantine icon brought to Venice by Francesco Morosini in 1672.

The wooden choir dates from the sixteenth century.

Among the other works we should mention the **Sacresty**: the great painting by Tintoretto portraying the Marriage in Cana is surely one of the artist's finest works.

There are also paintings by Titian, among them those featuring Old Testament Stories and in particular The Sacrifice of Abraham and David and Goliath.

Church of the Salute. One of the absolute masterpieces of Baldassarre Longhena, this is one of the most harmonious and well proportioned pieces of 16th century architecture. Built on an octagonal plan it is scenograpically articulated by facade projections and crowned with a huge dome. Opposite page, above: panoramic view of the Grand Canal, the largest waterway in Venice. It crosses the city in the form of a big inverted "S" lined with magnificent buildings. In the foreground to the left: Palazzo Cavalli Franchetti. It was built in Gothic style, but rebuilt at the end of the 19th century.

Below: Venetian gondolas.

Church of Santa Maria dei Frari.

CHURCH OF SANTA MARIA DEI FRARI

This was built at the beginning of the fourteenth century, to replace an earlier building which had been assigned to the Franciscan Friars. The building is in brick, with a facade divided into three parts by tall pilasters. In the lower section there is a single elegant doorway, adorned with statues. The campanile, with its trefoil windows in the topmost section, is particularly fine.

The interior is on a grand scale, and there is a solemn severity in the great columns supporting high arches. It has three naves and seven chapels along the end wall of the Presbytery. Along the lateral naves there is a further series of altars.

There are other works of great artistic value here; various funerary monuments were made by artists such as Tullio Lombardo, Antonio Rizzo, Bregno, Longhena. The monument to Antonio Canova, which the himself designed, is especially interesting and striking; it has a typical pyramid shape and is placed above a staircase; from a rectangular opening on one face, the Arts, St. Mark and Genius all enter to render homage to the artist.

CHURCH AND SCHOOL OF SAN GIOVANNI EVANGELISTA

The Church is of fourteenth century origin, but the transformations made in the seventeenth century have profoundly changed its appearance. Inside there are works by Domenico Tintoretto (a *Crucifixion*)

Marieschi (*The Last Supper* and *The Exaltation of the Cross*) and Pietro Liberi (*St John the Evangelist*).

The School began life as the home of the Confraternity of the Flagellants of St John, and it is one of the oldest in the city.

The little "campo" (courtyard) of the School is characterised by a marble decoration by Pietro Lombardo; the facade is fifteenth century and is in the Gothic style.

Inside, we find ourselves in spacious Renaissance surroundings: on the ground floor marble objects from the mediaeval period are collected and displayed.

A harmonious staircase designed by the architect Codussi (1498: he was also the designer of the doorway on to the Campiello di San Giovanni) leads to the upper floor, which was transformed in the eighteenth century by Giorgio Massari. There are paintings by Domenico Tiepolo, Sante Parenda, Longhi, Vicentino and Balestra. The altar is by Massari and the statue of St John by Morlaiter.

In the Oratory of Santa Croce, a church decorated with works by Bellini, Carpaccio and others, the "fragment of the Holy Cross" is preserved in a rich golden reliquary. In the Sala dei Convocati are works by Palma the Younger and Guarana.

Church of Santa Maria dei Frari: "The Asumption" by Titian. Among the many masterpieces present here, Titian's mighty painting of "The Asumption" above the main altar is certainly the most important. It is one of the great Master's most committed works: the sublime detachment of the Virgin as she ascends to heaven, the golden atmosphere, the vibrant colours, and the dominant red which takes its name from this great artist, have made this painting universally famous.

" *Enthroned Madonna and Child with Saints*": *a work by Giovanni Bellini.*
This one of the Venetian artist's most beautiful paintings. The triptych, placed in the sacristy of the Church of the Mari
dei Frari, makes its impact through the harmonious structuring of its parts and through his use of warm difused colours

CHURCH OF SAN ROCCO AND SCHOOL OF SAN ROCCO

The twin facades of these two buildings look out on to Campo San Rocco, and form a fine architectural complex with scenographical overtones.

CHURCH OF SAN ROCCO

The Church, rebuilt in the 18th century over a previous building in the Renaissance style, has a facade divided into two sections, broken up by Corinthian columns and deep niches with statues. The tympanied doorway is particularly fine, as is the bronze relief in the lunette (a copy of the original by Marchiori). The interior, with a single nave and a dome above the Presbytery, has works by Fumiani, Sebastiano Ricci, Solimena and above all Tintoretto. One of the major works by the latter is the cycle of the *Stories of St Roche*, among which perhaps the most beautiful is *St Roche healing the plague victims*.

GREAT SCHOOL OF SAN ROCCO

This is one of the most interesting of Venice's major architectural complexes. The facade of the building is in two sections, given grace and movement by columns with Corinthian capitals and large two-lancet windows. Built in the fifteenth century for the Confraternity of St Roche (San Rocco), with work by artists including Bartolomeo Bon, Sante Lombardo and Scarpagnino, it is the school which has kept most completely the cycle of pictures in its interior, the origins of which are in the work of the great master Tintoretto. The painter produced several of his masterpieces here, all characterised by deep expressive qualities. An important role is played by the mobile quality of the figures and scenes, and by the use of colour. The creative intensity which always typified the work of Tintoretto is particularly noticeable in this collection of paintings, which has even caused the School of San Rocco to be compared with the Sistine Chapel. The themes handled by the artist are those of the *Old and New Testaments* and are presented in about sixty paintings, both large and small.
The New Testament scenes include: *The Crucifixion* one of the most dramat-

ic and intense representations of the scene, thanks to the crowded canvas, the various perspective planes used for the composition, the strong use of shadow, and the explosions of light which make the representation especially vivid. *Jesus before Pilate, the Last Supper, the Prayer in the Garden, the Resurrection, the Baptism, the Nativity, the Temptation of Christ, the Pool of Siloam, the Ascension, the Raising of Lazarus and the Miracle of the Loaves and Fishes,* are the other titles to be seen.
The Old Testament scenes depicted are:
Moses causing the water to gush forth; Adam and Eve; God appearing to Moses; Crossing of the Red Sea; Jonah emerging from the belly of the whale; Miracle of the Bronze Serpent; Vision of the Prophet Ezekiel; Jacob's Ladder; The Sacrifice of Isaac; the Fall of the Manna; Elijah supported by the angel; Elijah distributing bread to the people; the Passover of the Jews.
We should also mention a Self-portrait of 1573, and paintings of St Mary Magdalene and St Mary of Egypt.
In addition, the Scuola di San Rocco also has paintings by Titian (*The Annunciation*),by G.B.Tiepolo (*Abraham among the Angels*) and Zanchi (*the Plague of 1630*).

Church of San Rocco and Scuola di San Rocco. A beautifully designed complex of great architectural interest. The School dates from the 15th century.

Some of Tintoretto's most interesting paintings can be found in the San Rocco complex. Above: "The Crucifixion". Below: the Upper Hall.

Church of St John and St Paul, better known by its Venetian name, San Zanipolo: it is one of the richest churches in Venice for works of art.

MONUMENT TO COLLEONI

The equestrian group is to be found at the centre of the Campo di San Giovanni e Paolo. It is one of the greatest of all masterpieces of Renaissance art. It was carved by Verrocchio towards the end of the fifteenth century. The composition is highly expressive in its moral energy which derives from the frowning expression and fierce pride to be found in the great condottiere's features.

CHURCH OF SAN GIOVANNI E PAOLO

KNOWN AS ZANIPOLO.

Together with the Basilica of San Marco and the Frari, this is one of the most significant artistic centres in Venice. The Church was built in the 13th century for the Dominican Order, and was only completed in the mid-fifteenth century.

EXTERIOR

Its typical features are the use of brick and the elegant simplicity of the Gothic facade. The lower part of this facade is broken up by blind arches in which funeral monuments have been inserted. At the centre is the great doorway, outlined by marble columns, the work of Bartolomeo Bon. The apsidal section is particularly beautiful; here the play of volumes created by the polygonal design is aided by magnificent double-lancet windows.

INTERIOR

This is divided into three naves, by tall columns surmounted by pointed arches. It is particularly rich in art works:
At the rear of the facade:
- *Monument of the Doge Alvise Mocenigo;*
- *Monument of the Doge Pietro Mocenigo,* an exceptional work by Pietro Lom-

bardo (15th century);

Right-hand nave:

- On the 1st Altar is the *Madonna and Child and Saints* by Francesco Bissolo, set in a carved frame of bas-reliefs.
- *Monument to Antonio Bragadin* carved by Scamozzi and dedicated to one of the heroes of Venice.
- 2nd Altar: a fine polyptych, portraying St Vincent Ferreri, one of the earliest works of Giovanni Bellini;
- Chapel of the Addolorata: this is in the Gothic style and was decorated with stuccos in the 17th century;
- Chapel of the Madonna della Pace, so-called from the Byzantine image of Our Lady on the Altar;
- Chapel of San Domenico; the roof of this chapel is dominated by the large painting of the *Glories of St.Dominic*, one of the best works by Piazzetta (1727).
- *Christ* by Alvise Vivarini;
- *The Almsgiving of St Anthony*, by Lorenzo Lotto (16th century);
- Chapel of the Crucifix: there are funerary monuments and statues in bronze by Vittoria;
- Chapel of the Maddalena, in the Renaissance style.

Presbytery:

- *The High Altar* is a masterpiece by Longhena;
- *Funerary Monuments* of Venetian Doges, among them that to Andrea Vendramin, the work of Pietro and Antonio Lombardo.
- Chapel of the Trinity: here there are a number of *tombs*, some of them pensile in design.
- Cavalli Chapel.

Left Transept:

Here there are Funerary *Monuments*: that of *Doge Antonio Venier* has carvings by Pierpaolo Dalle Masegne.

- Chapel of the Rosary: this is a treasurehouse of works of art. There are paintings by Veronese, depicting *The Annunciation, the Adoration* and *the Assumption*, and others by Bonifacio de'Pitati. In addition the Chapel contains sculptures by Alessandro Vittoria and Girolamo Campagna.

Left-hand nave:

- *Sacristy*: works by Bassano and Vicentino;
- *Monument of Doge Pasquale Malpiero*;
- *Monument of Doge Tommaso Mocenigo* (the work of Franco Terilli da Feltre);

Scuola di San Marco. The church faces on to the little Campo di San Marco in one of the most atmospheric spots in Venice.

Opposite page: *The Church of St John and St Paul: polyptych showing San Vincenzo Ferreri, (2nd altar): a magnificent polyptych by Giovanni Bellini, and one of his first works.*

- *Monument to Doge Nicolò Marcello*, by Pietro Lombardo,
- Statue by Alessandro Vittoria, portraying St Jerome.

GREAT SCHOOL OF SAN MARCO

A Renaissance building designed by Pietro Lombardo, and in the upper part by Mauro Codussi. It has an unusual facade in polychrome marble. The construction is assymmetrical, and has a large decorated doorway and pointed windows with tympana. The front is crowned with a series of arches of varying heights. In the interior - now used as the City Hospital - some of the rooms have fine wooden ceilings, formerly with paintings by Bellini and Carpaccio (these works have been transferred to the Gallery of the Accademia).

CHURCH OF SAN MOISÈ

The Church dedicated to Moses has a sumptuous facade in the baroque style by Alessandro Tremignon, built for Moisè Venier. The cam-panile still retains its fourteenth century features.

The interior is also baroque in arrangement and decoration. The paintings date mostly from the seventeenth and eighteenth centuries, though a few works are by Tintoretto and Palma the Younger.

CHURCH OF THE MADONNA DELL'ORTO

Opposite page: *Church of San Moisé. The ornate baroque facade covered with decoration and bas reliefs make it one of the best known churches in Venice.*

This is one of the most interesting churches in Venice. It is named after the statue of the Madonna inside, which is considered to be miraculous: it was found in a field close to the church.

The magnificent terra-cotta facade combines features of the Romanesque, Gothic and Renaissance.

The remarkable trefoiled loggia motive follows the line of the sloping roof with statues of the Apostles set in the niches. The ornamentation on the great doorway is of exceptional quality.

Inside, the three naves are divided by marble columns supporting terra-cotta arches. The church contains numerous works of art of great renown. Outstanding is the amazing panel by Cima da Conegliano showing *St John the Baptist among the Saints* (15th century).

We also find one of Tintoretto's absolute masterpieces : *The Presentation of Mary in the Temple* which he painted in 1552. Again by Tintoretto there are his beautiful *Last Judgment* and the *Adoration of the Golden Calf* (presbytery).

Above the altars we find works by Palma the Younger and Giovanni Bellini.

Church of the Madonna dell' Orto. Its wonderful facade features a marble loggia adorned with statues. Splendid marble decoration emphazises the doorway, the rose window and the jutting arches.

"CAMPI" AND "CAMPIELLI" IN VENICE

As Venice was built on a group of small islands in the lagoon there is a shortage of open space on the site. Almost all of it is covered with buildings. The little squares which still remain free of houses, palaces and churches are called "campi" (fields) and the smaller: "campielli". This is the case with Campo di San Polo, Campo Morosini and others, all possessing their own special atmosphere.

The one space which can be defined as a "piazza" is the Piazza San Marco, the world famous Piazza San Marco.

Left: *Campo S. Stefano*
Below: *Campo S. Maria Formosa.*

Campo S. Polo.
Campo S. Stefano.

The houses of Venice were built on islets in the lagoon. The city is criss-crossed by canals large and small; some of them, the "rii", are very small. This practically unique situation gives the city its unforgettable look.

The few streets (known as "calli") cross the canals over bridges of varying size.

The canals wind among the houses, reflecting ancient architecture and the elaborate decoration of the noble palaces.

The city is suffused in an atmospere of enchantment that makes it unique the world over.

Left: *One of the many "rii" of Venice.*

Below: *Campo San Bartolomeo.*

Opposite page: *An atmospheric corner in the historic centre of Venice.*

ENVIRONS OF VENICE – THE VENETIAN LAGOON

The Venetian lagoon is composed of a group of islands and places of natural interest which are a great attraction for tourists. It is also exceptionally beautiful. The Lido, and the islands of Burano, Murano and Torcello certainly have great appeal for the visitor as well as winding up his overall knowlege of Venice.

Apart from monuments of world renown there are spots where a few moments of peace and quiet can be found, as well as wonderful views and attractive comfortable beaches along the shores of the Adriatic.

In the pretty little towns and villages on the islands we can discover traditions that go back thousands of years and reveal the extraordinary skill and creativity of the inhabitants: the art of glass blowing is mainly practiced on Murano and is the most striking example of the work of master-craftsmen who have created an authentic art form over the centuries.

Then there is the lace-work of Burano, patiently and expertly produced by the women of the island: this too has become one of the most valued expressions of artistic craftsmanship. The Lido, the long island which almost completely closes the Venetian lagoon from the sea, is famous for its fashionable beaches, and particularly for its important cultural events.

LIDO

This is the name of the long strip of land separating Venice from the open sea. Two channels divide it from the other land barriers along the shores of the lagoon: the San Nicolò channel and the one at Alberoni.

The Lido is in the forefront of tourist attractions because of its splendid and elegantly equipped beach facilities, as well as for the important in-ternational cultural events held there.

Among these the **International Exhibition of the Art of Cinema,** or the Venice Fim Festival, must be mentioned. We also find here the Municipal **Casino**.

The Lido has been inhabited since the Middle Ages.

The **Benedictine Monastery of San Nicolò** was founded there in 1044. The small village of the same name has grown up around it.

The Lido is in easy reach of the charming village of **Malomocco** huddled around its small central square. It was founded in the 6th century on the opposite shore of the island by Venetians who were fleeing from invasion, and rebuilt a few centuries later on its present site.

In front of the Lido port stands the **Fortress of Sant' Andrea** built in the 16th century by the architect Sanmicheli.

Panoramic view of the Lido of Venice. The Lido is one of the most fashionable and elegant bathing beaches in Italy during the tourist season. It is excellently equipped with comfortable bathing facilities and has a long clean sandy beach.

Above left: *The auditorium where the world famous Venice International Film Festival is held.*

Above right and below: *some of the line of luxury hotels that characterize the Lido.*

MURANO

This is the best known of the islands in the lagoon and its fame comes from the production of exquisite glass-work which has reached an extraordinarily high level of artistry.

The craft of glass blowing has been carried out for centuries and in every period has expressed the consummate skill and creativity of innumerable masters. A Glass **Museum** documents this splendid tradition. A visit to the glass works completes one's knowlege of this ancient art which has been carried out under the most refined methods known to the craft.

The island of Murano is also fascinating for its churches and palaces which reflect the architectural splendour of the ones in Venice.

Particularly handsome are the Gothic **Palazzo da Mula**, the **Palazzo Giustinian** and the Palladian **Palazzo Trevisan**.

A visit should also be made to the Renaissance **Church of San Pietro Martire** where we can admire works by Giovanni Bellini (*Madonna and Child with Saints*) and Paolo Veronese (*St Jerome in the Desert*). There are very fine wooden dossals in the Sacristy.

The **church of Santa Maria e Donato** goes back to very ancient times. It was founded in the 7th century, but rebuilt in the 12th century. The apse is particularly beautiful with its double order of terra-cotta loggias whose arches are bordered with marble. The bell-tower is 13th century.

The interior of the church has three naves divided by columns with magificent capitals. The 12th century floor is paved with beautiful mosaics. Here we find works of art like the Pala of *San Donato* by Paolo Veneziano.

Like Venice the island of Murano has a Grand Canal of its own, flanked by stately buildings of the finest architecture.

Venetian lagoon: Murano. One of the best known and most visited places outside the city. Famous for the production of Venetian glass, it also has a number of interesting monuments to offer. In the photo we see the Basilica of Santa Maria e Donato.

Murano: one of the glass works which have made Murano famous all over the world. For centuries the production of artistic glass objects has continued a tradition handed down from one generation to the next.

BURANO

Burano is very picturesque with its pretty little painted houses along the small canals that intersect the island. Here we can find unforgettable spots with a charming atmosphere.

Burano has preserved the look of a typical fishing village. Fishing boats make their way along the canals that criss-cross the island and the nets are hung out along the embankments.

The island is really four tightly connected islets. It was populated when barbarian invasions drove the Venetians on to the lagoon where they found a place that was naturally sheltered and secure.

The fame of the island of Burano is linked to the production of lace which the women of Burano work with consummate skill. It is a tradition that has passed down through the centuries and finds its expression in products of exquisite beauty and elegance. Begun in the 16th century at the command of the wives of some of the Doges, lace-making has been cultivated with patience and a remarkable sense of artistry. The **Lace School** was created to preserve this art.

The 16th century church of **San Martino** well deserves a visit.

In the 17th century **church of Santa Barbara** there is a beautiful painting by Giovan Battista Tiepolo of "The Calvary".

Venetian Lagoon: Burano. The island has preserved a remarkable atmosphere of the past and is also famous for the exquisite lace proudly and skillfully worked by the women of the island.

Some views of the Burano lagoon with canals crossing the island.

TORCELLO

A delightful island in the Venetian lagoon, an oasis of peace and stillness. The **Cathedral of Santa Maria Assunta** dates from the 7th century and was rebuilt a number of times. Its architecture is a typical example of the Ravenna style. The facade is preceded by a narthex. Beside it we find remains of an ancient baptistry with an octagonal plan.

The interior has three naves divided by marble columns supporting magnificent 11th century capitals.

A great mosaic covers the west wall showing the *Last Judgment* (Byzantine work of the 12th century). The *Iconostasis* in front of the Presbytery is particularly fine: it contains 13 icons showing the *Madonna* and 12 *Apostles* and some sculptures. There is a magnificent mosaic in the vault of the apse showing the *Madonna and Child* (13th century).

Above: *The Venetian lagoon. Torcello. View of the island.*
Below: *Church of Santa Maria Assunta. View of the apse.*

Torcello: The "Last Judgement", a magnificent mosaic occupying the whole of the west wall in the church of Santa Maria Assunta.

GONDOLA

The most typical Venetian boat, long and narrow with the characteristic points at both ends. It is a little over 11 metres long, irregularly shaped to give it a particular tilt so that the gondoliers can row with one oar.

It probably originated in the 7th century, but its use did not become widespread until the eleventh.

From the 1700s onward, the gondola, whose shape had evolved over the centuries until it reached its present form, has had its measure, shape and ornamentation laid down officially, and it is built by master craftsmen who pass down their skills from father to son.

In Venice, the dockyard where gondolas are still built and repaired, has survived in the Squero di San Trovaso.

HIGH WATER

The "high water" phenomenon is one of Venice's most serious problems. The city was built on a group of small islands in the Venetian lagoon. Under particular weather conditions and because of a combination of elements - wind and high tides - the Adriatic waters rise and rush towards the mainland. This swells the water in the canals and they overflow, so that all the city streets and squares are invaded by "high water"; the first hit is always Piazza San Marco.